Reflection of

LOVE

A memoir of Hope

Minister DeVante R. Hill

Reflection of Love

Published by Devante Hill at Destiny House Ministries

Copyright 2016 Devante Hill

Table of Content

Dedication

To my late grandmother, Sharon Denise Brown, who showed me nothing but unconditional love in her time here on earth. Everything I know, I learned by watching you not live perfect but love perfectly. Thank you for being not only my grandmother, but my mentor.

To my late cousin, James Edward Jones Jr., who walk hand in hand with my daily as we both grew up until your demise, thank you for telling me that I meant something to the world when you saw firsthand how I felt and what I felt. Your love and brotherhood will never be forgotten.

To my paternal grandmother, Jewell Dowell, I vowed to you that I would have this book completed before you left the earth. Growing up, you would consistently tell me, that I have a ministry inside of me that would change the world. You would go on to tell me to write the book and share my story with those who needed to hear it most. Thank you for being my grandmother and my best friend.

To my parents, I love both of you equally and I thank God every single day for the personal battles we all have grown through. The person I have become can ultimately be credited to you two. At a young age I was created, but I wasn't aborted. Thank you for hearing the influence of God and not killing the purpose that would grow from the two of you.

<u>Acknowledgements</u>

To my amazing best friend, thank you for walking by my side for 6 very long years. You've been there when no one else has. You've seen the ugly times, the good times, and the amazing times of my life. No matter where I go, how life deals itself, and who I meet, you will always hold an amazing position in my heart as the voice of reason in the back of my head and front of my heart. Thank you for riding with me the entire time.

Forewords:

Apostle Benjamin Smith:

John 3:16 for me is the whole amount of God's sacrificial expression toward humanity. Life sometimes being a camouflaged, unapparent, and enticing pitfall; we lose our image of God. Devante, in this read, takes us on an excursion of resurrection, rediscovery, and restoration. Hymn writer James Rowe says it supremely clear: "When nothing else could help, Love (God) lifted me". Thanks for reminding us!!

Forewords:

Bishop James W. Thomas

Reflections of Love introduces the provocative challenge of introspection. This challenge, however, is one that leads to healing because once we move from pretentious love to authentic conversations about who we are and what real deficiencies we have, we are well on our journey to not only being better but assisting others in being better. Not every degree of transparency is for everyone but this book ministers to everyone on every level because it is the testimony of encountering transformational love and it opens the heart of mind to a God who both heals and delivers.

In addition, a portion of that journey

involves freedom from other people's opinion and the need for other people's validation. Capsuled in every experience is both a lesson and another mark of personal discovery. We survive the experiences of life because those experiences become a catalyst of ministry as we share that survival with others who, without our voice, may not survive. Reflections of Love is much more than just a book but a tool for helping others know that the power of God is so amazing that God can really heal us through His unconditional love. The same God that created us is the same God that strengthens us to be overcomers as well. It is my personal prayer that everyone who reads Reflections of Love will be encouraged and will embrace hope. In the words in one of the hymns of the church,

"Souls in danger look above, Jesus completely saves,

and He will lift you by His love, out of the angry waves.

He's the Master of the sea, billows His will obey, He

your Savior wants to be, be saved today. Love lifted me!

Love lifted me! When nothing else could help Love lifted

me!"

Prophet Willie L Mead

It is my honor and privilege to
congratulate you, Devante Hill, on the completing
and presentation of this book and its success. There
are many things I could say but the one thing I want
to say about you and your character in this very well
executed and exposed expression of truth in
relationship of you and your life, it will truly be an
eye opening discovery for many people. Yes, many of
us will be opened to see a bigger picture by hearing
the smaller parts of the heart of one. Because I have
been in a father son relationship with you for many
years, I have seen you from one extreme to the other.

I have seen your life expressions exculpate
from bad to alright, from better to good and from
great to the best. I have seen your ups and downs,
your quiet and verbal times. But in this part of your
destiny, it has taken me to another level of
understanding in more than one way and I believe

this will be the feeling as of many other. I say thank you for allowing yourself to be a vessel of God that can express and expose something greater than your life in the past. It is your future that is being developed! Here in the Word of God, which He has so eloquently spoken, God inspired words: "Love is patient and kind; love does not envy or boast; it is not arrogant or rude. It does not insist on its own way; it is not irritable or resentful; it does not rejoice at wrong doing, but rejoices with the truth. Love bears all things, believes all things, hopes all things, and endures all things. … 1 Corinthians 13:4-7 …. Yes, "Reflection of Love" … Your character in a book.

The Preface:

Love is found more than 131 times in the Old Testament and more than 179 times in the New Testament when reading The King James Version of the Bible. Love is so important that it is even legislated early in the scriptures of the Bible. It is a commandment for us to love God. In this popular religion and book spiritual practices, is it not strange that out of all the "thou shall not" commandments that the most important mandate, according to Christ, is the commandant to love? We can easily come to an astute conclusion that if we really and truly loved God, as He commanded, then falling in line with the rest of the commandments should come easy.

It is so important that we as God's creation grasp the concept that God is not a "Police officer," who arrests us at every wrong doing; however, He is the all nurturing father who has no other choice but to love because His identity includes love. We find in the scripture that love, or agape in the Greek language, presents itself in three entities within the scripture and our lives today. Love is a verb, as we find in Mark 12:31. We find in 1 Corinthians 13:4 that love is a feeling or an abstract noun. Last but not least, 1 John 4 informs us that God is love which gives love an identity.

Religion has bombarded itself with practices that imply solely a message of a convicting God as if He is a judge sitting on a bench waiting for you to deny his teachings. Religious conviction says that if you sin, God will condemn you and you will be doomed to hell, and the reality sets on those convictions being partially true but not effective for kingdom building rather than kingdom maintaining. Inadvertently, God is inferring his message of love. His message is a universal concept of an unapologetic and passionate love that derives from the beginning of creation. If marriages, families, and friendships could grasp this theory of God's love, divorce rates would decline dramatically, families would not divide over jealousy and minute issues, and friendships would go back to being long lasting. If we get completely lost in the love of God, the conviction of hurting him through sin would ultimately cause us to run back to him for repentance. What if we reached hearts and minds through the teachings of God's love instead of the "sin to hell" gospel?

Some scholars would argue with me and say that His law is more important to teach. In a recent theological debate, my passionate yet testimonial response was symmetrical to the scholar's, but with a different perspective. If God's commandments are what we live by as "Law" then the greatest commandment of them all was to love. I took on the philosophy that no matter what I had done, no matter what happened or who I looked like; God still in fact loved me. Even as diminished as my identity was, I still am the image of God. That mentality broke the chains off my life when I joined a thriving ministry in Memphis, TN, "Miracle Temple".

Apostle Benjamin Smith, the founder and leader, taught me personally how to invite God into my life and to allow God to move charismatically in a supernatural way. It was this ministry and its people who loved me regardless of what I looked like, that taught me to open up and Love God so much that his love literally drove a lifestyle of sin, incorrigible disease, and emotional pain completely out of my life. Now today, I am the reflection of

Love.

Introduction:

If you really want to understand someone then get to know their success through their struggle. God has, is, and will do more for us through our struggle than through our success. In fact, our greatness and the centralization of our success are both rooted within our struggle. Nothing ever just happens. No matter how hard we try to avoid the hurdles and turmoil of life, I came to find out that my human will is not strong enough to interfere with the divine will that God has planned.

If we look at the scripture we'll see that Jochebed, the mother of Moses, had to give him up to one of the longest rivers of the world because she could not protect him. Because of Moses's mother and her decision that we would call today "neglect" or "abandonment," Moses turned out to be a great leader in the presence of royalty yet carrying the spirit of humility, because He was really a Hebrew. In this read, I break down chronologically the decisions my parents had no other choice to make, based on their experience and who it made me into today. Your life is not chaotically confused because of catastrophic events nor is it distraughtly composed as a result of broken promises and empty dreams.

There is just a laborious process that God has to use in order for your story to resemble his glory. He needs to make sure that people understand when viewing your life that it was nothing and no one but him that rescued you, remodeled you in his image, and registers your name into the Lambs book of life. Your struggle defines your strength.

Struggle is intricate in helping you

appreciate the moment when you arrive to your destiny. It gives you vision and vision allows you to take something from your past and change it. I had to figure out a way to compose my life and what was a mess into a message of what God can do. The first thing I did was breathe. In life, you cannot get your next breath until you let go of the one you're holding. Navigate with me through each chapter of my life, as I break down my "Moses" experience and how my struggle defined who I was to become today. Chronologically, the Covenant came before the circumcision. God made me promises before the process of circumcision had ever occurred. I never had to go through to receive his promises, but the circumcision was just a part of the process.

Chapter One

Sitting here I feel the overshadowing presence of infamy for beginning this book as late as I have. I sense the heaviness of being behind, but I figured it is better late than never. I knew years ago that my life was not designed to be the conventional story of most young men nor could it be justified with explanation. My life, my journey, my story, and my past all come together to compel the hearts and minds of those who have been wounded, confused, broken, sick, stranded, depressed, and to bring the oppressed into the Kingdom love that God offers. The bible declares in Revelation 12:11 "And they have defeated him by the blood of the Lamb and by their testimony…"

I often times asked God "why?" Always wanting to know, yet it just never made sense that If

God really and truly loved me the way He declares he does, then how and why on an earth that he completely controls, would he have allowed me to endure and encounter the things that I could so indisputably recollect? I knew the ultimate conductor who controls the affairs of the globe was conducting this God given experience, but I still asked "why?" (deep breath)

The answer was simple and short… I can remember lying in my bed before preaching in Murfreesboro, TN in April of 2012. I felt the presence of God beginning to pervade my room in a way that was not all too unfamiliar. In him visiting, I could hear the Lord say "You have my love because you are my love." It did not totally make sense to me until I got to church that night. In fact, I questioned and wondered what the heck God was saying, because if I reflected over my life and every hurtful and painful occurrence that happened, I could not easily determine the presence of his love from my perspective. I was preaching a series entitled "Hell Date."

The series dealt with how we are subconsciously building a relationship with the devil and not even realizing it. Setting up a visible and actual dating scene to convey this message to a large group of college students, I explained how we can easily be gorging away at the lies and deceit of the enemy just because we are hungry for a void to be filled, while the enemy himself is secretly and maliciously trying to get into our spirits and taint God purpose for us. As most ministers can attest I begin to defer from my notes and flow in the spirit not even realizing that God was speaking directly to me.

Captivating the minds of the young people in the closing of the message, I could hear the sounds of about 40 college students on that Thursday night, screaming and yelling in tones of deliverance, "I'm free." My young, but older brother in the Gospel, who now was known as "Truth," stood against the wall in amusement of what God was doing that night in my life and how someone who was once a complete outcast on the count of my past private, alternative lifestyle could operate in the Glory of God the way I was.

Quite honestly, I had been preaching for some time at this point, but the way God presented himself in that bible-study was completely unfamiliar and amusing all at once. After everyone was resting in the presence of God grasping that in which they needed from Him, I began to feel a wrenching. That tugging was a battle between my spirit and my flesh. While my spirit was on a high from what was going around me, my flesh wanted exactly what the college students were getting while resting over the altar. In fact, my heart wanted Love. For the first time in my entire life, I felt a love that I've never experienced before. It was so surreal that it surpassed and drowned every previous hurt and obvious confusion of my befuddled past.

It all made perfect sense and it brought an appreciation of my present struggle. Why would God trust me with more light (Glory) when I cannot handle the current heat (opposition) that warms the light I have. The more of Glory I have, determines the opposition I'll face. So it was evident, that God wanted so much more for me, and that was why he was allowing me to endure so much heat. Understanding that concept, I became overwhelmed with the Creators matchless love in such a way that I began to just cry, as the hole that ached my heart for years had begun to be filled on that very night.

My connection with Love proceeded even further with my spiritual brothers Ryan and Tillmon who were on the cusp of birthing their poetic ministry and movement "Imperial Lighthouse". One night, they emailed me a poem that was entitled "I am Love" and it broke down my life molecularly and in totality. The poem set the tone for deliverance in my life. It was this poetic expression of deeply rooted pain and hurt overcome by the impenitent power of love that assured me that if I simply endure, my fantasies would one day meet up with my faith. The limerick illustration also reminded me of my not so distant past. Because of this poem, and that night, as well as my spiritual Hospital and church Miracle Temple, I am able to live my life in assured liberation and an

unapologetic love that I currently live in today.

(Poetic Expression)

"I AM LOVE. Because that's what God

designed for me to be. He created me in his image,

yet someone tells me I am less. Less than a man,

less than destiny, less than all that he has placed in

me. I am love. And God desires for me to have

greater things, yet my creator seems to have

forgotten about me. Maybe when he was spreading

his love he decided to skip me, maybe I wasn't

worthy of being blessed, now distressed in my

misery, my memory recalls that I am Lust. I trust my

life in the hands of a man. To touch the hands of a

man, was all my heart asked for. Man has blessed

me. He taught me how to be stress free, and as he

caressed me...homosexually, I just knew what to do next.

Now handing over my keys I realized that this man has shown me how to ignite the engine, causing my ignition to turn over and as I turn over, I realize I am Lust. And as my engine combusts I feel my heart beat, I just gave a MAN...yes! A MAN... all of me. And all of me is now with him. Now within him, I commend him for how he makes me feel. And somehow me saying Him and not Her was just a tad bit surreal but Not realizing I was making a deal with someone who didn't send me, yet he chose to befriend me because of what I could offer him.

A body...a body to convince society that in the midst of my decisions that it was right. I couldn't fight the temptation to be with what God didn't desire. But the Lake of fire was calling my name as my flesh grew insane it was then when I became numb enough to try and forfeit this game (suicide)...called life, all of this was calling my name (Not really able to tell the Pastor about my insecurities, only to hear him preach not about Gods love but my fleshly impurities. What salvation can that bring? Only to make me feel worse about who I am and across my mind came suicidal things.

He created Adam and Eve, yet I couldn't conceive the true meaning of this message. And within my confession I just want my people to understand I was lost. The cost of trading my soul for the pleasure of sin wasn't worth it. But feeling worthless and confused I gave in anyway. And every day, although convinced I wasn't right, I gave my body up seeking passion, in a fashion that was not to be displayed failing at hiding my secret I became dismayed and Although I prayed, around I still played and became a slave to what the doctor told me was HIV and in my unlearned mind it was Aids?

Prodigal son, Lord let me back in. I am willing to submit, even as a maid. And then I prayed...family prayed... and my faith stayed, and the Apostle spoke. And we spoke, and God's brush stroked and painted a picture of me I had never seen before. The "me" I had seen before was not this image that he painted in this picture. But when I stopped putting my mixture in his paint bucket, I could see my picture begin to change. Consider it strange, but the more of me I begin to let go, the more I became me. Now I feel free, I can express what He has made of me. Now I can see that once I was blind to the time, but now my image has been defined. Now I'm blessed to confess that the mess of thinking less, and being distressed, then seeking rest was all for me to find sight. Now in hindsight, I see that I have found life, and I found I am. I am who I am. I am a representation of I am and therefore I am a reflection of Love."

Living in the light of a reflection had its pros and cons, because my past made no sense to me. To my understanding then, if the beginning of the book didn't make sense then the middle nor ending would make any sense at all. That's exactly how I viewed my life and it wasn't until I received a breakthrough in the summer of 2013 that I was able to, in the words of Pastor Dexter G. Moragne, "Grieve, forgive, and let it go." I wanted so badly to understand my life and in doing so I had to confront it by tackling each suppressed memory, emotion, and pain one at a time and with each person.

Chapter Two

Most of my memories, going back, are mostly dark and a tad bit gloomy. I made the best of what I had with what I had. It was funny now to think that I was always the child who "stood-out". Not only did I stand out but for the most part I was bad as heck. My mother was very young, and to my remembrance we grew up together. She being 14 years old when she gave birth to me, I quickly realized that she would not always get it right. I can remember living in Michigan and being in a house with a man and his three daughters.

My mother had become very close to the young ladies while I, as a child, began to cling to their father who captivated me with a red guitar with white stripes. There happen to be one night that I'll never forget. This night would alter the rest of my entire life and would ultimately cause me to be whom and what I am today. On this particular night, this man, whom I really can't remember, touched me in a way that I would never forget even now as grown man. On this night I was violated spiritually, emotionally, sexually, and sooner or later psychologically.

I housed this experience and never really spoke of it. My mother being so young, her source of punishment then could easily be classified today as child abuse. I was terrified of her. I didn't know if I should sneeze, blink, or smell life when she came around. It wasn't because she was evil at all; the certainty of it was that she was so young and angry at her past. Adding a child to her circumstances was not the next life goal she had hoped for. In fear, I housed these emotions and fears of the "man with the guitar" and only spoke of

them to my grandmother who now resides in
Heaven. My mother and I vacillated more than
normal. Her being young and trying to find herself
and where she belonged in society, and me being
just a kid having to embrace all of it cause me to be
a bit smarter than most of the children around me.
My mother and I were never poor, but we never had
a lot of money. Growing up I can remember us
staying with one family to the next and the trend of
unstable environments inadvertently planted seeds
of instability in my life. One particular instance that
I can remember specifically would be when my
mother moved into what the citizens of Covington,
TN unwittingly called "The black folks projects."

We had not long ago moved from Martin,
TN and mother was building her own sense of
independence. In all honesty it was not bad at first.
My mother had started to become serious with a

man that I called "BB." She loved him so much and would move mountains for him, but the feeling obviously weren't mutual. He was such a dangerous man who physically and mentally abused my mother. She had at one time made it up on her mind that she was going to be completely done with him. Lying in my bed that night, I can remember being sound asleep with the fan in the window. I heard a small ruckus coming from across the room.

Being a scary six years old, there was nothing that didn't wake me up from my sleep. As I rolled over in the pitch black darkness, I could see my mom's now ex-boyfriend "BB" climbing through my window. His first response to seeing me was "ssssssh." I literally screamed to the top of my lungs in agony. My mom, who had not long ago gotten off work, rushed from the bath that she had been enjoying to see why her baby was screaming.

Again, there was a domestic battle between the two. From that night on, I was NEVER, and I HAVE never been able to comfortably sleep in the dark.

Living on that side, I had to learn to be tough. I was either that, or get whooped for lunch money every day. I had finally gotten started in school and in mid semester, my mom and I ended up at my aunt's house. My aunt Lisa was really my queen, as I called her. She was such a diva and to me she resembled the real strength of our family. Every time the need was there for my mom, Aunt Lisa was right there. Though she had a large family herself, she always had her doors open to anyone who needed help. As I got older I became more intelligent and had keen understanding as for what was going on around me.

Going into kindergarten, I began to spend

more and more time with my father, who at the time
was known around the city for his nice cars and
dating the best girls that the small town had to offer.
It cracks me up to this day to know that my dad,
who is now a Pastor, was such a hot commodity that
he had to venture out to other local counties to date.
In all honesty, he was a smooth guy, and I think he
used me for a chick magnet back in the day. We had
matching shoes, suits, and sometimes even similar
haircuts. Hanging with his side of the family, I
became a bit more acclimated with the church as it
relates to God. I had already been going avidly to
the local COGIC church with the neighborhood
grandmother. I was such a different kid that
everyone in a way adopted me into their own
bosom. The illustration and common saying that "It
takes a village to raise a child" played an intricate
part in formulating me into who I am today. My

father and his family began to pick me up almost every Friday after school to keep me for the weekend. To them, I was different, but in a way rough, because I had already began many of my life learning processes in a different and more hostile environment from the one that they had already instilled into my other cousins.

I was never able to really fit in at school. I could remember waking up every morning, after lying in bed aside my cousin Valencia all night talking about everything under the sun, even as a child. She would instill everything she had learned from school into me as if I were her student, and I would imbibe it up as if I were a sponge. Every Morning we'd wake up and make way to the bus stop to head to school. In kindergarten, I was so intelligent and insightful that the things my teachers were teaching, I already knew. Unconsciously, I acted out in such ways that I went through not one but three teachers. The first two being extremely strict and hard on me, while the other teacher had just started teaching and probably was among the sweetest of all the teachers I've had.

Ms. Kelli became more of a friend to me. She noticed how different I was as a child and she fed that drive to be different. While other students were on the rug learning to count, myself and another student were placed aside already adding and subtracting. When the other students were napping, Ms. Kelli allowed me to stay up and play educational yet entertaining games on the computer, while introducing me to country music all at the same time. It was her nurturing that ultimately gave me an escape from some of the parental turmoil I faced at home. My mother was surprisingly shocked that this teacher actually worked out. She quite frankly had been tired of coming back and forth to the school. She had tried everything from whooping me in the hallways, to punishing me at home by having me jailed within the four walls of my room. So to see that this teacher worked was a relief.

Moving into the first grade was a bit tough. By this time I had been with my dad and his family almost a complete summer and honestly didn't want to leave to go back to my mom's home for school. I probably gave my mom a terrible time during my first grade year. Sitting back now reflecting on those times, I realize how easy it is and was to just record everything I saw and allow it to come through my mouth and actions. I had become a product of my mother's angry past. I became violent, deceitful, and in a scary way at the age of eight sexual. I began drawing pictures of things that I saw and heard to only pixelate it within my imagination. I had gotten so intense that I drew my first grade teacher a picture of a completely naked woman on a test.

Ms. Knight, who I still know to this day, turned completely red in the face, and instantly called my mom. For the first time, my mother wasn't able to abuse me. She didn't even attempt to punish me. She cried. She cried tears of failure and what seemed to be desperation. My father's mother had one day showed up shortly after this incident to pick me up for the weekend. After my mother explained what happened to her, she turned to me and asked "Do you wanna' come stay with me Vante?" Not wanting to go for a better life, but more so to escape my mother's wrath before it came down, I immediately told my grandmother yes. Her and my father worked on getting me into a new school and ultimately worked on my way of speaking and living.

Living with my dad and grandmother, church and religion was a huge part of life. The pillars of the family were all built on faith. Every Sunday it was routine that my grandmother would cook breakfast, and we'd be off to Sunday school. I watched my dad become closer with God over the years until ultimately he decided to accept his call into ministry. He became so serious in ministry that when I got into trouble, he literally would beat the word of God into me. I'll never forget a long night of trying to learn the famous: Lord's Prayer" and my dad having tied three switches together and every time I would mess up, it was a few strikes to the legs. My dad, who will even vouch today, had some slight anger issues himself and when I would get into trouble, I would scream in such a way that my grandmother or grandfather would come into

the room and rescue me. The spoiled mentality that
I had was probably the result of their actions. I
never understood why he would force God on me
and make me become serious about God. I had
gotten to the point that I didn't want to go to church,
I hated bible study, and I disliked being forced to
read the bible when I had gotten in trouble. What I
did not realize was that my dad was planting seeds
into my life that I had no idea would one day come
back up from the ground.

Chapter Three

Growing up mainly around my aunts and clinging to my grandmother, having feminine tendencies weren't foreign to my character. Though I played sports and had peers who didn't resemble it, those tendencies were still there. Having a balanced household is something that I learned quickly was essential once I had grown up. Back then, living with my father and his parents is where I received all of my spiritual growth from, but on the weekends, I would go to my mom's house. Though she wasn't a bad parent, she just wasn't as spiritual as my father's family. What I have currently come to learn was that it is extremely dangerous mixing multiple spiritual cultures into a child's brain.

I have always been a smoothie lover. I

could go to the local ice-cream shop or sonic and mix all types of fruit and juice to have a mouthwatering taste of invigorating flavors. It always amazed me how all of those different ingredients could compose a taste that was so much different from the ingredients individually, but sometimes there were certain flavors, like bananas, that were more prominent in taste than others. For myself, I referred to my life as a blender. As a child, I would receive the spiritual growth from my dad's side and going to my moms, where urban music and an alternative lifestyle was accepted, I would also absorb that way of life. Going back and forth between households for many years blended a spiritual concoction and the results of it would later be poured into what I understood to be the real world.

Going into Middle School, my mother

had made it up in her mind that it was time for me to come back home with her. She had gotten on her feet and retained a local job and as a result she was moving towards total stability until her life was turned upside down. On one May evening, just before the summer had begun, my mother learned that her mother was deceased. It was this life changing event that sparked something different within my mother. She had never really had the chance to really squash the previous and past hurt between my grandmother and herself. Not being able to even say goodbye, my mother had to bury her then 49 year old mother.

Living with my mom from that point, in all honesty became hard. It seemed that what most of the children had the liberty to do, I really didn't have. The freedoms to go outside and have fun with friends, I missed. The liberty of going to sleepovers, little league games, and swimming parties, I wasn't afforded. In fact, most of the summer of 2003, after my grandmother died, I spent babysitting my younger siblings or just couldn't go outside for the sake of something happening to me.

I really don't think it was laziness that kept my mommy from allowing me to be a kid. I really think based on her experience as mother, she was afraid of her children being put in harm's way. Not only that, but me being the oldest of four, not to say that it was the right thing to do, but I was sometimes the only baby sitter that she had or could afford. I kind of grew into a bitter phase because of it while still harboring feelings being fondled with as a tot, not to even mention the only person who knew my secret was now deceased.

Something so traumatic happened in 2003

that would change my life, for the rest of my life.

My mother had already been quite physical with her

children, not because she was evil, but it was just

the only way she knew to get her point across. I

must be honest; my grandmother was no Marry

Poppins to her either. Seemingly this generationally

cursed mentality of verbal and physical abuse

carried itself down into my mom's way of thinking.

I will never forget a night shortly before my

birthday while living in Millington, Tn. Staying

virtually nowhere from the Navy Base, the

apartment complex named Flag Manor was right on

the corner of Navy rd. My mother had been gone

for almost two days, to this day, I am not really sure

where but my twin brothers and I stayed at a

neighbor's house who lived in the complex. Late on

the second night, there were no adults present in the

home. Now living in an urban community, things

like weed, alcohol, etc. were all common and at this point I was no stranger to it.

With no adults present and a house full of both teenagers and kids, there were two neighborhood teenagers that I had known to be trouble were trying to get into the house to enjoy the freedom of there being no adults. The baby sitter, who wasn't there, had a son who let these teenagers in. With me attempting to be the responsible one, I immediately tried to force them out of the house. With no adults present, and the neighborhood teenagers being older, they grabbed a hold of me and took me into the back room and did things to my body that I had never thoroughly experienced before. On that night, at the age of 11, I was raped.

Finally being released from the dark room where the unthinkable had happened, I began to cry and fight the teenager with all I had. At the time, being of small construct, there was just only so much that I could do. While fighting, I ended up calling the police. When the police came, of course the adults who were not present were the ones who received the most backlash from the police. My mother later arrived that night after a surprisingly unexpected phone call about the police being called. Living in the hood, the focus was not on "why the police were called" but more so "the fact that you called the police to my house." When my mom walked in the house, I never got the chance or opportunity to tell her what had happened to me because she immediately hauled in on my face as if I were a grown man.

On that night, as my mother beat me, my emotions shifted mid her punch. My feelings went from being in fear of my mother's anger to being afraid of death itself all in one night. It seemed as if she picked up whatever she could get her hands on to treacherously thrust it with all of the hurt, anger, and fear she had within her to my flesh. At that very moment my mother was no longer my mother but she successively had been taken over by a greater force that suppressed her will, but still remained an instrument that God had no choice but to use so that years from that day, He would be able to use me in ways that I would never be able to articulate. Most of our experiences have absolutely nothing to do with ourselves.

In fact, a great portion of my experiences that I did not bring upon myself, were essential in me being able to formulate a transparently raw testimony that the people could overcome by as the scriptures suggested in revelations. The reality is that there is nothing that you can do about it. Your human will is not and will never be strong enough to change God's divine purpose for your life. Be it bad or good, there is no dry season without a greater reason. So in one night, I was beat up physically, abused sexually, torn emotionally, and broken spiritually, abandoned adolescently, and confused catastrophically. Though all of this happened, I still yet remained covered supernaturally. The small light of God that I knew had been demised by the overshadowing darkness of that night and the phases of emotions I had to endure, but I would soon find out that the penalty for being chosen would sometimes be greater than the penalty for those who are only called. On that night, it was evident that I was chosen.

If things were not already bad enough, once my mother finished me, mortal kombat style, I was rushed to take a hot shower. Physically bruised and whelped at two thirds of my body, I can vividly remember the scares burning in ways that I can never explain. I am not sure what really hurt the most between my actually body, my feelings, or my spirit but the integrated pain of the three were unexplainably excruciating and those pains had no ending that night for what was to come. Getting out of the shower, my mother met me in the bathroom and began to go at it once again for a failed responsibility to my siblings over the course of her absence for two days.

As I put on my clothes, I had and prepared to make way to the car to go to my aunt's house. It was as we rode in the car that my mom threaten to send me to boy school and military camp for the sake of the behavior that she felt at that time was inexcusable. At this point, I was in my head thinking that it would be totally fine to be at one of those camps versus dealing with the mental,

physical, and emotional agony of being her son. Out

of my mouth, while sitting in the backseat of the

car, I yelled aloud "I'm going to tell my daddy!"

I'm not sure where the rush of emotions came from

or what propelled me to even say it, but what would

come after, I had never expected.

Once my mom had finished reaching in

the backseat from the driver seat to "touch" me, she

instantly gave me the green light to let him know

because he was not my real father. Now I have to be

honest, out of all of the beating I had gone through

that night, it was this verbal jab that hurt the most. I

mean honestly, I could have ended the night with

the belts, cords, punches, slaps, and even the broom

stick, but it was the uttered affirmation that the man

of God that I thought was my father for years and

years and years to come was not my biological

father. The man I emulated and loved and wanted to be like did not share the same blood as I. As I prepared to take rest that night, barely being able to breathe from my nose, I cried. I had no idea why or how God could have allowed such horrific things to happen to me by someone I loved the most. Tears began assiduously meeting the bloody scars from the results of my night.

Chapter Four

The following morning, my father had come to pick me up and dropped me off with my grandmother. I had never been so happy to see their face, but the results from last night both physical and emotional were hard to hide. As I met up with my grandmother, the first thing she asked about was my nose. Following her examination of my nose, she noticed the bruises and scars of my face, arms, and eventually my back. She immediately called my father back and they promised my well-being at me telling them what happened. I knew what type of trouble my mother could have gotten in for what she had done so I tried to protect her, but at some point I had a break down. My grandmother and dad both took me to the hospital where it was discovered that I had a broken nose. Out of nowhere came this State Trooper with his digital camera and notepad. My greatest fear even at that age, were my siblings and being broken up and away from them into foster care.

As a child, I took so much heat from many of my maternal relatives. It seems as if many of them had a preconceived notion that I was a troubled and spoiled child that they wanted no parts in. From family trips, holidays, and even sleep overs, I was never invited to but only by a select few of them. Growing up, I took it so personal and over time I hated myself over it. I would cry almost every single night. I felt ugly because I was treated like the ugly duckling. My self-esteem had fallen to a place of inexpressible sadness at the thought of me just not being good enough to fit in with a majority of my relatives, especially at them hating to see me coming for what they understood as to what I did to my mother.

My siblings ended up with other relatives and after classes and counseling, my mother eventually had the liberty of getting them back, along with many court dates and obstacles. I often times wonder what they think or thought of the entire experience. It took years upon years to realize that no matter what, I did the right thing by telling what she had done, but I was far too ashamed to let it be known that I was raped all in the same night. Going through a nasty court battle, my un-biological father and his mother were able to have custody of me once again. Though I had the world handed to me while living with my father's family, there was a void that was just empty and anyone else filling it would be impossible.

From neglected birthdays to overlooked

Christmas days with no phone calls, it seemed as if I had no mother in one season of my life. My grandmother and aunts had made strong attempts to fill the void that in all actuality only my mother could fill. There were moments, out of my sheer disappointment, that they would catch me crying as it relates to my mother and begin to highlight all of her imperfections. Though they were just speaking out of hurt just like I would, it was still my mom and I loved her. I always wanted to maintain optimism at her efforts and retain the mentality that one day she'd come back to show how much she loved me. So whenever they'd part their mouths to speak negatively about my mother, it pushed me away from them emotionally to the point that I felt disconnected from every one.

Here I am, in middle school and my mother has shown no signs of love for her oldest child of four. My father, whom I loved with all of me, is not my biological father, and not to mention his family appeared to despise the thought of my mother's efforts to be a mother in my life. I felt so misunderstood and lonely at times. Out of all of this frustration, my father's dating life was coming to a close and he had begun his quest for marriage. Upon marrying my now step mother, I resented the fact of having a step mother. Not only was I extremely protective of my father, but I also did not take kindly the thought of someone coming into my life trying to take the place of my mother, and for the most part she didn't. In fact when she initially conjoined to the family train, she was more of a friend than anything. We had tons of fun and often time made weekend outings.

The first year my father and step mother were married, my maternal mother decided to purchase me a slip and slide for my birthday. Now be mindful that my dad and his family would invest in Jordan's, video games, bikes, toys, trips etc. but the fact that this slip and slide came from my mother, it made it that much more special. I will never forget me leaving home on my birthday, and as I pulled back up with my grandmother, my cousins and step mother were all outside sliding on the slip and slide that my mother had bought me. I must admit that I was a bit spoiled, so as they slid and slipped I began to pack what was mine up because no one (me) had given them permission to open it up.

My step mother, (shocked at my actions) decided to come into the house and attempt to give me a spanking. As grown as I was, I picked up the phone and called not only my homie (grandma) but I also called my mom unknowingly creating a heated relationship between the two. From that point on, it took some time to warm up to my step-mother completely. She attempted with all of her might to be that mother that I not only deserved but needed but I remained steadfast and rebellious at only having my granny and mother in my life as mom.

My dad and step mother began to grow in God more and more as time had gone by in their marriage. As they grew, I had no choice but to grow and I really enjoyed it. My dad had left his home church, where had had been ordained minister, to become active within another local ministry. The church was all my family knew. My aunt had taken me, in the summer of 2006, to her home church in Moscow, Tn. The church was called Temple of Praise Church of God in Christ. It was not a big church at all but the missionaries there, including my aunt, would pray in ways I had never experienced.

That summer, what was supposed to be a vacation bible study, turned into a deliverance service. One of the missionaries there had no clue who I was but she called me to the altar. She whispered into my ear that I was special to God. She told me how much god loved me and how it all happened for a reason. She said that the Lord told her to cover me in prayer and to build a hedge of protection around me for what was to come. She instructed my family to cover me in the blood and in prayer because of how special I was in the eyesight of God. As she grabbed the bottle of oil, there were four missionaries who made their way to the altar. Evangelist Keels took the bottle of oil and turned it upside down on my head covering me with it.

As she prayed, I could hear the other missionaries proclaiming "Fill him Lord" and "Fill him for his purpose." As they prayed, my instructions where to simply cry out the name of Jesus. As I cried out "Jesus," my tongue began to do the abnormal. At the age of thirteen, God filled me with his spirit with the evidence of speaking in tongues. It was an experience that I'll never forget. The entire ride home, I spoke in tongues uncontrollably. At this point, I had a gift that I knew nothing about.

Chapter Five

Having friends and mentors from all walks of life, religions, and denominations, I had so many different interpretations of what the spirit was and how speaking in tongues played a part in it. It was later that year that God began to align destiny steps for myself and a few astute men and women of power to come into my life and shape me for what was next. That year, a major prophet had come into the city to do a revival at my local church. Though I was rooted in the Baptist church, being filled with the Holy Spirit opened me up to all of Gods many gifts, offices, and fruits so I knew what a prophet was, yet I had NEVER experienced one. Prophet Willie Mead came into town from Arkansas deep into the fall season of the year. Never meeting this man or knowing anything about him, after his sermon about the "Gifts of the Spirit" he called me up and said nothing though he hugged me. This hug was no ordinary hug. He wrapped his arms around my head and entire body and embraced me as if he were my father/mother.

As hard as I tried not to, I cried tears I did not even know existed. Prophetically, Prophet Mead saw a root of both hurt and confusion and by way of the power of God, He was influenced to simply hug me. He never said anything until after the service. After sitting down with me, my pastor, and father, the Prophet let me know that God sent him into my life and at the time he wasn't even sure why. He gave me his card to assure that I call him at least once a week to check in. Before I left to go home, Prophet Mead looked me into the eye and said "You have to give her over to God son." What he didn't know is that something was broken on that night.

After a few weeks of my parents speaking with him briefly, Prophet Mead and his wife both invited me to their home for a few days. God began to propose a special work for Prophet Mead, as it related to my life. We sat up all night long and talked about absolutely EVERY thought in my head. He dealt with every emotion one by one that I had buried into the inner crevices of my soul. Dr. Mead found those roots that had not even broke the ground yet and tried to pluck them. Through my transparency at the age of 13, the man of God was able to prophetically see the struggle that was to come so he embraced me and tried all he could to keep me from it. His ultimate desire was to protect me and keep me pure but that was only possible through my honesty and transparency.

My first time visiting him in Blytheville, Arkansas we went straight to church so that he could complete some work before service. Me being drained, I laid on the couch in his study and dozed off. In my sleep, I began to dream or relive the moments of my last abusive encounter with my mother. Sleeping and crying at the same time, Prophet Mead watched me as I toiled in my sleep, soaking wet from both tears and sweat. Once he had come to a point that he decided to wake me up, it was clearer to him then, that I needed him in my life. Dr. Mead began to construct a relationship with me much like the one Paul and Timothy had. Prophet Mead, who was later named "Daddy Mead," had a driving desire to assist me in surpassing every major obstacle that Satan had placed before me to distract me from greatness. He saw the anointing and power of God in my life in such a way that God allowed him to see what my struggles had the potential to turn into. His only stipulation was that I be honest with him and He would always be there.

As I got older, Daddy Mead became one of the most influential males in my life aside from my father. He was really the only voice that I would hear. The older I got, it seemed that I became even more sour towards life and everyone who was in it. I could not stand my dad for simple reasons. I genuinely didn't want our relationship to change and it didn't until he and his wife gave birth to their new son who carries his name. I became bitter because in my head, the baby and his wife were taking my place. From that, came not only bitterness and jealousy but hurt. I often times think back to the realities of those days so that I'd never be upset about it.

My father was young. He, my mother, and

I all grew up together. Can I really be upset that a 14 year old and a 17 year old duo raised me the best way they knew how? Though I couldn't be mad at them, the world was my only outlet to be angry. My teenage years, I felt so misunderstood and quite honestly I felt ugly. I never heard my mother in the pivotal years say "Son you are so handsome!" I cannot ever really recall my dad referencing young women and or how to treat them yet alone get one. From these experiences, I learned that it is so important that you are not only in your child's life but a part of it.

My father was not absent, however he was not a part of my life and today, that's ok because I was his first child. We shy away from the reality that the first child is the trial and error run. It is the simple things that really meant the most such as showing up at a track meet, or coming to eat lunch with me when the time was available. For some parents, it is just hard to balance extra time into a schedule, so active conversations can be just as supportive. "How was school?" "Did you have a good day today?" "You doing ok in you classes?" I never really heard any of those things. I lived in the house, but I was not a part of the household until I had gotten in trouble. All of it pushed me to be ok with being alone and figuring things out alone. Now my father was not completely absent to where it would make him a dead beat dad. In fact, his disciplinary efforts were commendable even to this day. When the time came, my dad moved away from physical whooping early on simply because my mom had already in a sense numbed me through that. He tried a different approach that I honestly think can be accredited in formulating me into the ecclesiastical pioneer I am today. The Lord's Prayer was something that I grabbed before any child in my circle. I remember kicking a deacon at church who was handicap early as a child. My father came home from church and not only whooped me but he made me bath and learned the Lord prayer. Every time I messed up, I had to go into the corner and stand for an additional 15min. After some time, my father grew weary of the "Standing in the corner" so daddy took a different approach. He intertwined a few switches and EVERYTIME I messed up it was a 15 second deliverance on my legs with those switches. Quite naturally, I quickly learned the prayer.

He was quite the same in my teenage years, without the switches! I would get into trouble and I would have to go read proverbs or a major chapter therein and compose a complete paper over what I read and explain it to him, It honestly was the most annoying thing in the world, but I am so Godly thankful at his attempts to raise me under the will of God. As sour as my feelings were then towards he and his wife, my attempts to get out of his house were stronger and stronger. Daddy Mead had become the only voice of reason. When they needed to access my heart or my mind, they would have him to interact with me. For some time it did work, but when I became hip to what was going on, my transparency with Prophet Mead began to change, and as my transparency changed, his ability to really help me diminished.

My hurt of not having a strong mother figure and lacking the relationship from my father that I desired, ultimately sent me on a quest to find love. At that point, I would have taken love from anyone that was not associated with my family because in my head, God had let me down as it relates to a parental love. In high school at this time I was dating a young lady who was a pastor's daughter as well. She didn't live far from me, so our relationship was stronger than just going to school and meeting up, but it was not until I found out that she was no stranger to a few young men while she was telling me she loved me that I was able to find myself deeper in hurt that I could articulate. No one knew or understood the amount of hurt that I felt. It seemed like I inadvertently had the worst luck as it relates to love coming from women. I didn't understand why she would do me such a way, or why my step –mother seemed to treat me like cinder-Vante, and why my mother did not show any signs of wanting me. It was those roots planted deeply into my soul that would sprout the next phase of confusion in my life.

Chapter Six

Somehow my summertime visits to my mom ended up turning into me staying with her and I must say that the transition from the country life to the city life was quite difficult to transition into. In addition to that, I suffered a major culture shock while transitioning from a school with mixed culture and ethnicity to an urban school that was predominately black. Moving with my mom in the summer of my 9th grade year had to be the worst decision I could've made, not because I had a bad mother, but I had the spiritual food that I needed to continue to groom into the man of God I was becoming. At this point I had already begun experiencing my spiritual gifts and I was coming to know and understand my purpose and calling. Going back and forth between my mother and father in those stages broke open a familiar passage that I had experienced at an earlier moment of my life. That blended life that I once had was now manifesting itself again. I went from spending the week at my mother's where the atmosphere was not as religious as it was with my fathers. Then I would go and spend the weekend with my dad, I was in an atmosphere that wasn't liberating to my flesh either.

My visits to my father on the weekend began to diminish as the summer came closer simply because my dad lived 30 miles away, and at the time, He just felt it was too far to drive every weekend. My mom began to allow me to work with her fiancé at the local market, in the meantime, just to have some additional funds in my pocket. Some weekends had gone by and I noticed how I gradually transformed from being able to live a life that exemplified Christ to uncontrollably becoming less spiritual without any control. It seemed as though, the less exposure I had to a Christian environment the more I had become less Christ like. Please don't get me wrong in my writing. I am not saying that it is impossible for one to be spiritual without church, but my point is that it was impossible for me to be as spiritually inclined as I was while being exposed less to God. I vividly remember telling my aunt that I wanted to go to church with her on a particular Sunday. She came and got me early that morning and we traveled to Moscow, TN to her church. There I experienced two things that I had never really taken part in. The first was a concert with a major Gospel artist. After the service, this particular gospel artist made his way to me when I was alone and looked me into my face, shook my hand in such a weird way.

Walking away from the encounter, I felt

as if this man had undressed me with his eyes, and I honestly was not too sure how to deal with it. I had never had a conversation about the birds and the bees with my parents. The talk of how relationships and courting works was never described to me and talks of homosexuality were mixed. On one side of my family it was ok and accepted while on the more religious side it was frowned upon and not even tolerated. I walked away from the church and hopped in the car with my cousin and I said to her "I think the Gospel artist was gay..." She looked at me and asked me how I came to such a strong conclusion. Trying to avoid explaining feelings and emotions that I really wasn't too sure about remained hard to do so I shifted the conversation as she took me back to my mothers.

When I got home, I had to put some extra thought into what happen so that I could get a clear and concise understanding on what I was feeling. Thinking and wondering why he would look at me in such a way, and why this old man would shake my hand as if he was attracted to me were all questions that raced my mind. I didn't know if I liked it or hated it.

With those thoughts and emotions festering, I started at my new school, Whitehaven High. The students there were quite different from what I was accustomed to. In all actuality, I initially hated it. Honestly, my perception of the school I had grown to adore, was tainted by color. I formulated an opinion of the school based on the popular demographic of people I saw not knowing the educational power the school possessed. I immediately became active in the chorus at the school as an outlet to the shift of atmosphere that I endured at home.

My mother's house was not terrible, but it was quite different from living with my dad and his family. In fact, she orchestrated a tightly structured household with my younger twin brothers and I. There were no going outside and extracurricular activities after school were farfetched. Every morning, it was my duty to wake up for school and to ensure that my sibling got up shortly after me to get ready for school so that we could get there on time.

After some time of being a student there at my new high school, I became exposed to a wide range of spiritual activity. In particular, homosexuality seemed to be a presence that undauntedly chased me everywhere I went. Seemingly, at my new school, the boldness that came with this particular stronghold, became forever scarier. Young men, in the same grade as myself and higher, openly participated in homosexual activity and it seemed as if I was being involuntarily recruited because of my level of curiosity and lack of male influence. As the days had gone by, I noticed a shift in my spirit, and an incline in my flesh. I became more comfortable with my surroundings, and the "LIFESTLYE" was privately formidable for me. So much so, that I became, with shame, what the church would call a male whoremonger. From skipping classes and sneaking home, after school meet-ups, and even sneaking out of the house at night, I was so exposed at a young age to the lifestyle of homosexuality, to where it became difficult to pull away from it. There was one instance that would change my life forever. I had become serious with a young male at my school, and every night that my mother would leave or go back into her room, I would sit on the phone with him until we'd both fall asleep. One particular night, I feel asleep rather early and the phone died. Let's be very clear, it was not my cell phone but it was my mother's phone that she would let me use just while she was away. I had fallen asleep on the phone and the battery had died. This young man called back and left a voicemail. It was this voicemail that would play a pivotal role in my entire life.

My mother grabbed her phone the next morning before I could even wake up and see the notification of a voicemail for myself. I could hear the screams of my name waking me up from my sleep…. "DEVANTE!!!"……. "DEVANTE!!!!" The first question she asked me was "Who is this?" Pressing play on the voicemail button, I was almost afraid to even answer her question, but I knew that the next 2 minutes that I had to think of an answer to the next question would make or break my experience. She followed with "Are you gay?" I had no idea how to answer. Standing there, my legs began to shake, my fingers twitched, and my head began to throb. But this was my moment to make a real choice. I boldly stuck my chest out and said aloud to my mother… "I don't know!" Now looking back on that day, I laugh at how funny my response was and how afraid I was in that moment.

My mom had a history of being quite abusive as a result of some unresolved anger from her past, but in this instance she said nothing for three whole minutes. She looked me clearly in the face and said nothing. As bright as she was, redness from frustration filled the crevices of her face while pervading the pressure points of her head. She said nothing, and I honestly think that is what scared me the most. She opened her mouth and out came not a curse word, but randomly she just said "Get you clothes on so that you can go to work." After spending a day at work, I can vividly remember coming home and distinctly smelling my favorite meal before I had even walked into the house. I could smell the aroma of brown pinto beans, cornbread, and white rice all together.

As I walked into the house, mamma stopped me in my tracks as I quickly tried to make way to the back room. She looked me into my face. I could see she had been crying and the hurtful confusion was obvious on her face. She, in all actuality reserved every right to be confused because she had no clue where it had come from. To think that her oldest son was completely confused about his sexuality is enough to drive every mother into frits. She assured me in that moment of just how much she still loved me. My instructions were clear and concise. She didn't approve of my life style but she never damned me either. She simply just didn't want it around the house.

Though religious believers and faith based families would have immediately went into prayer and probably would have stripped life away from me, I am so glad that at the time my mother didn't do those things to me. In fact, I am sure it would have been my father who probably would have snatched phones, privileges, etc. on the count of me having a struggle.

It was my mother's response that ultimately confused me a little. She never called me out of my name. My mother never judged me. She told me what the Lord said about living a life of homosexuality, and really moved on from the subject. I am sure it took her days and maybe even months to get over it, but she never loved me differently.

Chapter Seven

It was then that my mother and I built a relationship on trust. Shortly afterwards, she introduced me to the Davis Family YMCA right beside my high school. It was there that I met Ms. Sabrina Norwood, who instantly saw the anointing on my life upon meeting me. The YMCA became my home away from home. When my mother really wanted to punish me, she'd snatch away those privileges to be at the YMCA after school and I would straighten up quickly. I had no direct plans on going to college until I reached the YMCA. The group I was a part of was known as the "Teen Achievers." From college tours to field trips, my stay at my mom's house became pleasant because by this time, I had created friendships, developed rapports with teachers/principles, etc. The only thing that I missed was church and I even got that from the Choir at Whitehaven High School and even at the YMCA I found myself surrounded by the spiritual kids at times.

My being liberated in truth after telling my mom about my lifestyle but bound by what I knew the word of God implied about it cause a huge imbalance in my life. Some days I'd be perfectly happy and other day's sadness would be my alarm clock. I consistently remained thoughtful of how much I missed the presence of peace, joy, and God's spirit when being with my father and his family. While even writing this project, I often times remembered that my mother did the best she could as a young mother with children on her own. Some days she had no clue how we'd eat, lights would be on, or how she'd clothe each of us as the seasons changed, but somehow she made it happen.

Unswervingly dealing with hardships at home, I found myself weak in spirit and I began to decline both academically and emotionally. Seemingly at the time God knew exactly what I needed. I needed friends. Somehow, in the midst of my lifestyle and low social class, I managed to befriend not only my homie Desmund but also Kevin, who would eventually go on to be a lifelong brother. Desmund and I were two peas in a pod. Every single day, he and I both would hang out before and after school. Sometimes we'd even skip class during school. To be honest, I learned how to dress from him. He showed me the potential I had. Unknowingly he built a monster.

Not being able to mix outfits as much, I went from nameless uniform tops, dickies khakis and old chuck Taylor's with holes to Ralph Lauren, Steve Maddens, etc. I would call my Aunt Peggy and dad almost every week asking for these shoes and that outfit, and by the end of the week they'd have it at my doorstep. Sometimes my dad would drive 40 miles to come see me and drop it off himself. I'm not sure if I was more excited about the package or the money I'd get from him when he came. Becoming more and more poplar at school and at the YMCA, I began to love living in the city but I hated going home to the turmoil and hardships.

As Desmund, Kevin, and I became an unbreakable trio, I became more transparent with them than ever. They cared nothing about my struggles, hardships at home, or anything that anyone else had to say of me. They were authentic friends that I genuinely needed at the time. I can remember coming home on one instance and there was mother sofa being tossed over the balcony. Shortly after the couch, tossed over the balcony was every article of clothing I had. We were being evicted. I had so many mixed feeling and emotions that I could not formulate it all into words. My mother was not even there, nor my younger siblings. The lady who drove me to school every morning held me tight and told me "God is doing it for a reason!" For some odd reason I believed her and my spirit began to change.

Out of the window peaked so many of the neighbors. It was honestly by far one of the most hurtful and embarrassing things I have ever encountered or had to deal with. My mother, being determined to put on courage and keep going, pulled up and had already had a plan. In a matter of two hours, we were moving to another apt. Most of the stuff she was totally ok with leaving there only because the apartment was infested with so many roaches. While most saw an unbalanced and unfit mother, I saw strength and tenacity. I watched her pack clothes and cry all at the same time. She loaded mattresses and pleaded with God all at once.

I knew that moving wouldn't be so bad. I found myself in the mix of older men in the apartment complex. Late nights when my mom was asleep or even out on the town, I found myself out of the house in abandoned apartments and in what I called "The Dark house" which is where they lived. I knew these men meant me no good yet the fleshly pleasure that came from visiting seemed to be unshakable until one of them did something that would scare me for the rest of my life.

The night prior to being evicted, I snuck out of the house and over to the "Dark House" and met up with one of the residents I had encountered on multiples times before. He went on to tell me of how I should go and get checked because of him finding out that he was HIV+. Imagine being 16 years old and being told you could potentially have HIV. Afraid out of my mind, I totally ignored it the next day and ended up being slapped with the reality of being evicted that evening. The following day, after moving into the new apartment, I knew in my mind that I wanted to die. It was that day that my friends began to ask me "Are you ok?" I got to the YMCA and Ms. Sabrina could see brokenness on my face but I couldn't say a word. The next day I skipped school to go and get tested. The results came back negative but the spirit of depression and suicide still ate my flesh alive. It was Desmund who decided to pray for me, and Ms. Sabrina who would go on to talk me into a real deliverance, while

Kevin would come behind to assure me of who I was and that I was loved. I would normally talk to my Grandma every day, directly after school, and for almost a week she didn't hear from me. From my mother's eviction, to her job displacement, she seemed to be more frustrated than normal on a day to day basis which caused me to be even more depressed. I'd be slapped around for not having the dishes completed, punched for not having the bathroom cleaned, etc. My life had taken a toll for the worst. On multiple accounts, I can remember drinking bleach, taking a hand full of Ibuprofens, etc. with expectations to die from it.

I woke up the following Sunday and decided to put on the only suit I had and make way to the church I had seen so many times riding to school. I walked to Miracle Temple. I knew nothing about the church. Had no clue who the pastor was, yet alone any of its members, but I was so sure that if I made way back to what I knew then I could get the spiritual help I needed. I walked to the church broken, bruised, and battered because life was and had always been in shambles for me. As I walked in, I could hear the sounds of an angelic choir singing "Even Me.'' I believed that the service was designed by God just for me. Apostle Benjamin Smith would get up to preach on how God was about to turn things around.

From the first Sunday to my last Sunday there, years later, I never walked back to church. At the first service, I was taken in my multiple families including that of Apostle Smith. Elder Maurice Thomas and His wife would speak so much life into me and pray for me when I couldn't pray for myself. Ms. Pam Finnie and her husband would become like God parents to me. Her brutal honesty would break chains on my life in ways that couldn't even be worded. Ms. Johnson would link me up with her son Christian and her family would later make me their own. I am fully convinced that had it not been for the first Sunday of me getting to Miracle Temple, I would not be here today.

Every service pushed me higher and higher into God's undefined love and caused a conviction to be birthed within me that I didn't even ask for. I really wanted to live for God at this point. My demeanor changed. The way I carried myself shifted, and deliverance started to take place. I became active in the choir, youth ministry, and even dance ministry. After some time, God had completely changed my life. I felt as if I was back to the young minister I once was in God. I can remember going to the Apostle and speaking to him about getting back into ministry as I once was.

Chapter Eight

Life had a way of getting better as the time had gone by. Life seemed to be pretty smooth as long as I strived to live right. I had become known at school as "Preacha' man" because I always walked the halls preaching and singing. I somehow found happiness in the middle of the stormiest time of my life. Even now when I hear people reference the familiar passage of scripture in the book of Matthew 8, when Jesus was sleeping in the boat while it was storming, I often times get irritated at the apparent omission of the miracle that the savior was resting in the middle of the storm. Could it be that God doesn't want to deliver us out of the storms of life, but giving us peace and rest in the midst of it would really emulate his presence and glory in our lives?

My relationship back then had become extremely close with the DAVIS family YMCA and I had even become employed as a life guard. My best friend Kevin would evolve our bond from friendship to brother hood. There were occurrences that would take place at home and I would be able to come to work and talk to him about it with total security that my issue would not leave the barriers of our friendship. People often times commend me on the loyalty and dedication that I offer each of my friends, but it was really Kevin that taught me true friendship. He taught me that no matter what you are, who you are, and when you've done it, we all have a story. Even with a present struggle of my sexuality, lack of the best clothes, etc., Kevin, being hetero, never changed and in fact he showed me how to be a real friend.

My time at Whitehaven was drawing near. I can remember my mom, on my way to school one morning, letting me know that I was to go live with my dad. I am not going to lie, I was so angry. I had finally gotten my life on track. My church family loved me, my school loved me, and the YMCA had become my family away from home. I simply was not ready to be catapulted back to Tipton County so fast but I had no choice and the change would be quick and abrupt. I can remember my dad coming to get me, which was rare at this point, and we debated on me staying with him versus my grandmother. I have to be honest and say that I earnestly was not feeling the entire move, yet alone moving in with both my dad and step mom.

As my dad continued to purchase a new home, I started at Brighton High School living with my grandmother. Brighton High School was so much different from Whitehaven High School. When I walked into the doors, it was almost like a culture shock. There were people of every walk of life. From Asian to Caucasian, Brighton High School had it all. I had quickly gotten with the process of Brighton High School and the structure of discipline thereof. Among my transition, I was met by the guidance counselor who would assist me in becoming acclimated with my new schedule, curriculum, and teachers. Ms. Moffat not only became my assigned counselor but she also filled the role of my very own personal psychiatrist as well. There were days that I struggled tremendously to transition with the culture as well as with the expectations of my new instructors, and she would be right there to sometimes pull me out of trouble as well as tighten me up in her office. Ms. Moffatt could see the emotional distress resting in my eyes on a daily basis and quite honestly it began to take a toll on how effective I was at school. I can remember days of going into her office and just crying my eyes out at how unhappy, unstable, and quite frankly unsupported I was.

I had grown into strong liking of Brighton High School. The faculty and staff absolutely loved me. From the lunch ladies, to the principals, down to my teachers, they all loved my vibrant personality and eccentric spirits that I brought to the classroom each day. Eventually, I grew so fond of school, that I would be excited to get there and away from home. While attending Brighton High, I started working and matriculating into adulthood. My first opportunity came from the local McDonalds. I was so excited not only because I was able to make my own income but the food options multiplied now that I was an employee. As a high school student, the dollar menu was my best friend. I worked at McDonalds for almost a year up until it was time for my senior year's homecoming and I was already set to get off early so that I could attend the festivities. The on duty supervisor chose not to let me leave on time, even though I had already been there 6 hours. I kindly took off my apron, removed my hat, as well as McDonald's shirt and remorsefully instructed the manager to take those things and go to hell in a basket of French fries. My mouth had only become that smart because I quarreled often with my father and really couldn't say the things I wanted to say to him so I released them elsewhere. Not to mention, I already had another job set up with Pizza Hut literally two doors down.

Leaving McDonalds that night to celebrate my senior winter homecoming with my friends was exciting and yet it had taken a turn for the worse. After the game my friends and I all went to Memphis to a trampoline facility. It was awesome and unexplainable fun to feel like a kid again with people who genuinely cared about me and our skin color wasn't the same. While there, my blackberry kept ringing and when I had finally answered it, a voice was on the other end that rambled "Preacha' man, you must be on my end?" It was the same Gospel artist who I had seen years prior and gave me eerie feelings. From the indirect and subliminal messages on Facebook, I often times felt like the guy was just weird but me lacking guidance and constructive influential relationships, I was naïve enough to respond with "Yea man… I am." After leaving the inflatable trampoline facility, I ended up meeting with the Gospel artist at the gas station and trailed him to a set of apartments. With all honesty, everything seemed platonic and we were just goofing off. He and His best friend were both there so I felt safe and as if things were ok. As frail as I was, if anything had happened, I wouldn't have been able to help myself.

As the clock begin to tick at a later time, I noticed that it was moving closer to my curfew. As I make way to the door through the kitchen to get to my 87 cutlass sierra with a bad steering wheel and no horn, the man cut me off and started singing "Where are you going?" in the scariest melodic way and quite honestly it freaked me out completely. So sadistically exclaiming my desire and need to leave, He wouldn't let me leave out of the door but instead grabbed me and pinned me against the wall to make attempt to complete his voluptuous yearnings on me. Going into deep detail, would probably turn the stomach of the readers of this project but I can honestly say, the 45 minute ride home was the longest and saddest that I had ever driven. For the second time in my life, I had been sexually abused and the God that I so desperately worshiped was nowhere in sight. In fact, one of his servants, one of his melodic voices of worship helped minimize who I thought I was into who I didn't want to be.

Oddly, I noticed my tendencies had begun to change. My father and I would argue so bad that sometimes I wouldn't even go home. My grandmother's home was my escape route. I was so emotional and lost. Confused would be an understatement. By this time my father was Pastoring and had a growing church that I loved, but in essence loved Miracle Temple more. I couldn't fathom seeing my dad, the man I argued most with, as Pastor. It wasn't a good balance. So luckily, I had family they would rescue me on both Sundays and

Wednesdays to attend worship at Miracle Temple. When I would get with the Chaney's be it with the Mother Chaney, Papa Chaney or their daughter whom I called sister, I would feel like the little kid that I never had the opportunity to be. The security of a father I received from Papa Chaney was indescribable. The love and nurture of a mother, Mother Chaney would deliver both with her heart and with her pots and pans. Alisha, their daughter, would be like a big sister to me. She would keep it real with me even when it hurt. She loved me no matter what. Alisha would often times see my tendencies begin to change and she would never judge. She would probably tilt her head to the side like a confused puppy and just say "ok" But she protected me. She fed me and nurtured me the best she could with what I would allow her to.

Life had gotten to the point that my Dad

and his wife had their side of the house, and I had mine. I walked in from school, spoke, and went back to my room and didn't come out unless I had to work. Pizza Hut introduced me to real work ethic. As a server, some nights, I would run the entire floor all by myself. Football teams, baseball teams, and church groups would come in and leave big tips for me and all I had to do was greet them with a smile. My Algebra teacher's husband happened to be the General Manager, and they loved me like a son. It seemed like everyone who I came into contact with, from this point, would begin to adopt me as their own. As the summer approached, I began my second job at the local sears as my hours would slowly fade away at the decline of in house dinning at Pizza Hut. I was so use to money that I decided to do both Sears and School Aged Child Care while finishing my senior year of high school. I had officially moved to a place of complete independence. My life was ok with the exception of my terrible rebel against my dad and his wife. My mother was MIA. I had no clue what was happening with me emotions and sexuality and with no one to discuss it with, whatever emotions they were simply grew into themselves. I started dating this young lady right before graduating. She was the first girl I had really ever dated. I was so into her but she couldn't really have a boyfriend at how strict her parents were so we snuck to sonic and Walmart to see each other. It had gotten to the point that my life aside from her became too much and to keep from hurting her it was best to let her go. My dad and I quarreled as graduation and prom came close. At the time, he was so focused on my spiritual edification that my academic progress didn't mean as much to him at the time. So having to enroll into college, pay for senior dues, prom, etc. became so much. Out of nowhere comes mentors and father figures who pushed me into greatness.

My mangers from Sears were a local couple who went and purchased a local store and not only hired me but mentored me. They would give me money off the table and invite me to dinner whenever they saw fit. Dr. Thomas Carruthers was a local OB/GYN, and He would mentor and foster me into just making good decisions no matter what. I learned from him that when you were dealt lemons, make lemonade. My biggest supporter would be my grandmother. She pushed me to make it happen. I would call her sometimes and even go over to her home and just cry at how unhappy I was with my life. She'd be the first to say "Baby, you've been through so much, but God has something in store for you if you keep trusting him" So at the latter part of May, in the face of every struggle up until then, I graduated from Brighton high school with my father no were in sight and my mother outside the building from running late. They missed the announcement when all "Future-servicemen" were asked to stand. I was hurt that night, so I earnestly just wanted to be alone. I left the high school and went to the Mississippi river that night and cried till I contemplated jumping but there was something on the inside of me that just wouldn't let me give up. I left a week later for basic training. Only to return right before the summer ended to start at the University of Memphis as a freshman.

Chapter Nine

Starting at the University of Memphis was a complete last minute decision, in fact, I enrolled while in Basic Training for the United States Army. By the time I had gotten to the campus, I was bitter with my parents, confused about my identity, and sure of my anointing. My abrupt welcome into the world of independence met me before I could honestly prepare, so I winged my way through it.

I drove onto campus in my 1986 Cutlass Sierra with no airbag and a bad power steering. You could hear me coming 10 miles before I had even gotten there. Packed in my vehicle, was not only the things I had purchased for my dorm room, but the belongings of my friends both Nigel and Chris from my church, Miracle Temple. We were set to go to the same school, staying in the same dormitory building. Luckily, Chris lived right beside Apostle Smith and praying over us before we left was mandatory before we pulled off. I vividly remember, while he prayed, apostle made mention of Grace. "God even though you saved them, when they go astray, cover them with grace and love until they come back to you." I'll never forget that prayer.

Life at U of M was impeccable. I attended classes, made it to every auxiliary meeting that I was a part of but something was still missing. While there, I was solely independent and had no resource of finances. No one would hire me at the glimpse of my school schedule, so I was left to attempt to figure it out. In me figuring it out, I became intertwined with the wrong demographic people. Mainly older crowds appeased my interest the most only because they would contribute most to my needs. I was so lost and desperate for help. I'd go to churches and the Pastor would call me up with attempt to make a pass at me. It became so bad that I did not identify as gay or even bisexual. I hated it in fact, but I needed help so in my head, I went with what was easy to attain. It became so bad that I would be pulled ten different ways after classes at those who were trying to strike my attention. Some were abusive physically, others verbally, and a few sexually.

What hurt the most is that these were Pastors! Not just some local storefront Pastors but major and notable names in my local city. One of them had become so attached that he would rent one of his homes to me in exchange for private companionship. So here I am, young, naive, dumb for help, and living at the every beckoning call of a notable man of cloth in the city.

Having only interactions with Pastors and honestly people with money, I had every reason to identify myself as an escort. I gave so much of me out that I didn't have much left to myself. I'll never forget sitting in the classroom and my phone rang almost three times during class while taking a test.

The teacher took my exam and put me out of the classroom because my cell phone was a distraction. Not knowing who it was calling me, I instantly grew frustrated. Whomever it was they left a voicemail. "Mr. Hill, this is Ms. Jackson at the Shelby County Health department, we need you to give us a call as soon as possible please." She left her number as well as the address. Thinking that this was a joke, I googled the phone number and sure enough it was the health department. I called my cousins and friends, thinking it was a sick joke. A few days had passed and my grandmother, who was my primary address, told me that a sheriff and a woman came looking for me. Frantically nervous, I called the lady back. Her first words very sharp, direct and to the point. "Mr. Hill we need you to come in, you've come into contact with someone who has tested positive for HIV/STD. My heart immediately dropped as my entire life, in my head had flashed before my very eyes. I went home and cried, without even being tested myself. The mere fact that my reality had encountered such, drove me passed being sane. I had crossed paths with a devil I was not prepared to wrangle even with my undeveloped anointing.

The next day, I made way to the clinic. Because it was my first time, I can very distinctly remember my exact experience. The air was crisp and dry with the smell of underprivileged individuals who didn't take grooming as their first life priority. The signs were old and the floor was blemished. I went into the office and signed my name explaining who I was to the receptionist. There I saw men, women, and everything in between in the waiting room. Coming out of the back, were two individuals and the woman had begun to fight her boyfriend because he had passed something along to her. There was little to no discretion. The nurse case worker called my name to come back to the examination room. I made way to the back with my heart fluttering in both anticipation and fear that today my life could be completely different.

Ms. Jackson asked me a series of questions in the examination room about my sexual behaviors. It was so awkward answering them back when she got into genders. My stomach turned because I knew I really hated my habit but I just merely wanted to survive and it all just got out of hand. My heart began to beat as fast as it could, as the anticipation grew. The nurse came into the room with these huge manly hands and two needles along with other tools to obtain blood samples. She reached into the counters to grab, what looked to be long Q-tips, for STD testing. I already had a strong fear of needles and had no idea how to explain that to here primarily because I could get past how huge her hands were. I let her know from jump, "Ma'am, now I'm just going to let you know off the top that I don't really do needles." She laughed as if in her head she was saying "Well you gon' do needles today"

The pulled the blood from my arm and swabbed my mouth and other unpleasant test protocols only to make me go back out into the stinky waiting room and wait almost 2 hours. Ms. Jackson called me back into the examination room because my results were finished. The look on her face was quite blank, so I really could not tell what the results were from her facial expression. She started to talk and the only thing that I can vividly remember to this day was this. "Mr. Hill, your results came back positive for HIV virus..." From that moment, I cannot explain how blank I had become. She talked and talked and talked became more and more lost in the bottomlessness of my deepest fear.

For me, my military goals and career was over, If I ever wanted to have healthy children then I'd run the risk of transmitting it. If I ever wanted to get married, what woman would want me? My misery became lost in my uneducated understanding of realities that I was not even abreast to think about. I can remember leaving the office that day and heading straight home. As I got there, I noticed the locks were changed. The doors were locked and my key wouldn't work. I called the landlord who happened to be a Pastor. He explained to me that he had a reason for changing the locks and that I'd need to meet him at his church office. Quite honestly the pastor was merely a friend or one that someone my age would call a mentor. Our relationship was never really odd but odd things happened.

For example, after hours is when He'd hit me up to check on me. Or if he was on campus, He'd let me know to meet up with him and talk about simple things such as class and life. But for him to lock the doors on my place was just honestly scary. When I got to the church office, I noticed He was the only one there. Knocked on the door and he swiftly opens it. His first words were "Hey, you hadn't seen my church have you? C'mon let me show you around!" as if that was my reasoning for coming. I was already depressed at how my day had gone thus far, and this negro had the nerve to change my locks with no notice and then invite me on a tour of his large but old rusty edifice? I grew irritated. As He's chowing me his church I'm noticing that He is showing me more and more odd places in the church. Like why do I need to see the basement? As he took me down and showed me a basement kitchen, a deep and dark spirit just crept its way into the kitchen with us as I walked in.

I never physically saw it, I never heard it, but I could feel it. I could feel it breathing down my neck and I could see it in his eyes. The notable Man of God who I trusted as a friend as a mentor opened his mouth and said "Come Here." I'm, in my head, battling on what I should do. Should I take out running at the thought of him catching me or shoot…. This man has the keys to all of my stuff. So my response was outwardly "For what?"

His voice tone shifted and He confessed to changing my locks because He wanted me to "come here". I had to think quick on my feet and come up with a demanding response yet not a rude one. I told the Pastor that I had to go to e meeting for one of my classes and it was for a grade. I just came to find out why my doors were locked.

He sat the keys on the counter directly beside him and says "Come get the new keys. I had to change the locks to make sure old tenants did have duplicates." Me, still not understanding why I had to come over to that side of the kitchen to get the keys, walked over to him to get the keys. The closer I walked, the more it felt like that evil presence was growing more and more over my back. I tried to keep from walking to far. I tried to lean as hard as I can forward without getting in arms reach of the suit wearing wolf. He did not move. He just looked at me and watched fear in my eyes in not knowing what He'd try next. Once I got the keys, I began walking to the stairs to make way out of the kitchen, out of the basement and to my car. The oddest words came from his mouth and I knew then that this world and the church itself was corrupt. He asked me to come minister at his church.

Respectfully declining, I grew more in fear of him after that interaction. Once I got home that day I laid in the bed and wept. I cried until the wetness of my tears drowned the pillows of sorrow that were supposed to support my head in the event that I needed to rest. I wanted to die. I made way to the kitchen and started to just take every pill I had from anti-biotics, to 800 MG Ibuprofen. It was so hard because the reflection of my life from that point to birth just didn't seem to reflect the love that God not only has to give but promised me as a child. I didn't get how my childhood could be so screwed up. I knew my parents meant no harm and they had to learn how to be a great parent. But to me that wasn't my fault. I didn't understand how I was approached in the church and no one said or saw anything. I didn't understand why I was abused and never heard an apology for it. Me being raped 3 times by the age of 18 became the forefronts of my mind.

My life was built on the premises of what I could offer a demographic of men who, if anyone knew what was happening their entire empire would fall. How did I get myself tangled in such a life that the rest of my life would now be so screwed up? I took pills…I'd go lay down in the room and… I'd take more pills praying that I'd fall asleep and NEVER wake up.

That same week, my church would be having a Miracle Healing and Deliverance service. That night I skipped and didn't go of cores only waking up in the middle of the night screaming at the appalling abdominal pain developing in my stomach from all of those pills. I made way to the bathroom and just began to gag until everything inside of me came up. I cried out to god in my bathroom floor.

My cry was no theological hermeneutical expression that was well thought out and arranged with presentation. No, my cry was simple. It was desperate, and it was transparent. My cry was "Help me God." I knew I couldn't go to anyone in my family, I had to convince them that I was ok and that with or without their support I was going to make it. Part of it was pride and ego while the other end was the fact that I didn't have much moral support from the two that it mattered most and that is because they were learning to be parents.

To this day their relationships with the siblings after me can show that they learned how to do it with me and it was a bit easier the second or third time around. I could go to the church because seemingly everyone was to NOT be trusted. The men and women of god would either talk about me or leave me just as abandoned as I already was. I vomited and threw my hands up crying out to god for help.

The next morning I got up and I felt empty as a box of crackers that had been ransacked my church mice. My face was pail as if I were already dead. I resented the fact that I had actually awaken. Didn't have any money and lacked gas. I walked to campus and found myself in the office of Ms. Gillard. She had such a spirit that would invite the MOST ABSOLUTE lost person to her. Not really knowing her deeply other than in passing. We somehow started to talk and found ourselves on the way to lunch. I'm nervous, and knowing I had no money, I went into a full praise when she mentioned she was taking care of it. We sat and ate outside on the balcony of the UC and she began to just witness to me about life and some of the things she struggled with presently. Leaving the table I was able to be transparent and honest about where I was and where I needed to be. That night I made it to Miracle Temple where the Miracle Service was taking place. I sat outside my car and cried looking at the results and how I had to go back for retesting and counseling not to mention referred to an infectious disease doctor.

I started and made way into the service and I could hear Miracle Temple singing one of my favorite arrangements. In one harmonic voice, I heard the falsetto toned sopranos singing "Even me Lord, Even me. Let some drops now fall on me." I made no stop at any seat, but I went directly to the alter and laid there with my results crumbled in hand. I can remember Pastor Kelly, the associate Pastor, and Apostle Smith both praying for me in such a way that it's as if they already knew.

The other ministers had no idea what Apostle and Pastor Kelly were warefaring over but they immediately showed how well trained they were by joining in prayer. As they prayed, I could still hear the heavenly sound of "Even Me Lord,

Even Me. Let some drops now fall on me….."

Somehow I don't remember much after that.

Honestly I just remember waking up in my bed and

three members from church were in the house along

with a peer of mine who often stood in prayer for

me. They all prayed in my house and one of the

mothers came to me and said from her mouth

"There is a spirit in this house, and you need to

move. No, there is no driving it out because the

owner of the house is the one that hosts this spirit."

The scary thought was that the pastor was the owner

of the house and I had just withstood odd events

from him. I woke up that Friday morning with two

missed calls from my Spiritual father.

When I returned the call, his inquisitive

nature went prophetic and already knew that today

was the day of my last testing and counseling. He

went with me and we waited for two hours for the

results to come back. In the meantime, the praying that occurred in the room would rally up enough angels to bring healing to the entire clinic.

Initially, I was broken about it. I was unmoved either way. I had already been tested twice and this third time just didn't seem possible or logical to expect anything else. So to hear the Man of God pray and declare and decree things that didn't seem to be possible was pointless for me. He prayed and stopped to rebuke me. His words were simple. "How can you preach and prophesy, shout and speak in tongues, dance and declare over everyone else's life but can't team up with faith to heal your life.

Regardless of what you did, who you did it with and how you did it… God still loves you son and He still has purpose and Destiny for you to fill.

The process of changing your life won't happen overnight. You are going to fall, but He'll give you grace under repentance to get back up gain. His mercy loves you. His favor follows you. Trust him for healing.

The young lady came back in and looked as if she had seen a ghost. Her response was a bit removed from faith but still lacked a concrete understanding. "Mr. Hill, don't get alarmed because there could have been an issue with the test but these results came back negative" In her attempt justify, she was interrupted with our faith and reasoning as to why God did what He had done.

She attempted to get me rescheduled but I was quite adamant on being tested shortly afterwards. They drew blood from the other arm. She called me two hours later to let me know those results were negative as well and that it was concluded that I had a "False-Positive." In essence, a false positive is a medical way of saying to me "This is your warning for you to get back where I need you to be and focus on your purpose." To this day, now 6 years ago, I will go monthly just to remind myself of my encounter with God, and the results have and always will be as long as I can help it, Negative....

Chapter Ten

Life after my results became better. I had some sort of support system. I had spiritual mothers and father to pop up being a part of my life. I knew my anointing, I just needed a raw experience and to be healed by love in order for me to really overcome and evolve into who God has called me to be. From that moment forward, I lived my life, in the assured favor of God based on his love for me, in situations I had never expected to get out of.

God showed me his love. He allowed me to rest in the dearest place so that He could prepare for me a table in the presence of my enemies. There were people that would come into my life after these events and show me such a love that I needed in that season. The reality is, God would have, by this time, given my dad and mother the tenacity to be all that I needed them to be, but based on the past, my pride and ego just wouldn't allow me to go back. Though I had forgiven, I had not forgotten and I held on to that.

There were spiritual influences that God would give me that would usher me into the next season of my life. For example; while being lost in the sauce of life, I met a guy named Dre. Now he would come off to as this huge big armed muscle man with dark skin causing the average person to be eerie of his capabilities, but his heart is one that can never be unmentioned. Dre would eventually move me into his beautiful home and foster me not based on what I could offer him but based on what I could potentially evolve into. Dre became a father for me when I couldn't go to my father for understanding. Most of the time, I didn't want to be agreed with, but if I could only gain some understanding, things would have been better. God literally expressed his love for me through Dre. No matter how many times I had lied to him, hurt him with my actions, he continued to love me as a son. There were people who wondered why he would keep trying to work with me at how much of a lost call I was, and how he would never let go of my hand.

So much time had passed by and I found myself on track with God. I noticed my walk made more sense. It made sense for me to get out of Memphis and that's what I did. I found myself in Nashville, TN and it was only by chance and not by plan. From getting approved for the apt complex, to the drive up, I had no clue what God had in store for me. I moved there because it seemed that God was moving in the city and I wanted to be in the midst of it. Upon my arrival to Nashville, TN and getting settled, a few friends and family had started having weekly bible study in the apartment complex. It would be so powerful that the numbers would multiply weekly. We'd experience God in such a way that the most lost would have no choice but to find him. Young ladies rededicating their lives back to God, men crying out to God for deliverance, even some were filled with the gift of tongue. The way He used me in those moments, I knew I was in my purpose. I knew I was in place and in position but I didn't understand at that time how just three years ago, I was still anointed but lost. The movement grew in such a way, that a local pastor, Elder Roger Russell, wanted to have it grow through his already established church. The church was amazingly beautiful for the area. And the people there were equally as beautiful in spirit. They allowed us to have free reign to move as charismatic as we'd like just as long as lives were changed. We evolved from 6-7 young people to having registered upward

150 young adults to our youth and college ministry.

For me, I became more baffled when some

of the same people I partied with, were the same

ones who were at the alter screaming in tones of

deliverance "I'm Free." It was a pleasure for me to

go back and God would allow those who knew how

I use to be, see and experience what God was newly

doing in me. I became so serious about my calling

and my ability to move under the fire of the Holy

Ghost that I enrolled into American Baptist

Theological Seminary. Mixing my Pentecostal

charisma with the powerful theological background

of the Baptist church, was a mixture that would set

my life a sail for the rest of my life. It was like

adding biblical truth to Pentecostal power and it

made me more astute in my presentation and more

passionate in areas such as social justice and

community development.

Pastor Russell and I wrestled with each other but we learned to learn from each other. I could be transparent with him with where I was and he'd continue to foster the imperfections in me while cultivating the gift at the same time. It was as if God was qualifying me for ministry along the way. God showed himself in every collegiate bible study we had. We'd get started around seven and would plan to be out by nine, however, most of the time the Spirit of God would come in and we'd just be locking the church up around 11:30. I never made anyone stay but I was willing to stay as long as it was needed to make sure whoever was there got what they needed from God. That is what compelled them. That is what caused them to bring a friend the next time

I evolved more into who God was calling me to be and less into who I wanted to be, I had to learned balance. I could never go and beat up and condemn a person living any lifestyle that I had ever participated in, because I could understand where they were and I knew how to pour love into them, to cause them to come out of those dark places. My old friends never disrespected my idea of wanting to be closer to God as it relates to my life, only because I never judged them as my heart began to change. Not only did these relationships develop into brotherhoods, but my level of effectiveness with them, as it relates to their spirituality, was strengthened because God could trust me to witness to the hurt and not try to manipulate them into my own personal weaknesses be it perverted or hatred.

I learned to be transparent. I learned to allow

my light to be my witness by being there for those

who the church would probably over look. It was

like all those years of preaching in pulpits had gone

down the drain because my new desire was street

ministry. If I really planned on meeting and being

able to witness to those who the church will never

reach because of its stigmas, I had to be available

and not have my heart and mind so set on being

"saved" that I miss the opportunity of evangelism.

My biggest fear was trying to understand how God

could use me and my reputation and my past not so

far behind me and not to be played with in the black

church.

God began to educate me on how his love

works and how he operated, not religion. The Lord

brought me back to the scriptures in which he had

two commandments that were most important to

him. Even with missing and messing up all of the

"Thou Shalt Nots" when you master the most important "Thou Shalt" your life will begin to align even more. His greatest commandment was to love him. The second greatest commandment according to scripture would be to love others. It is amazing how we declare to show God our love through laborious preaching, sanctified dancing, powerful praise, but we don't love God enough to change our ways no matter how simple they are. What if the body of Christ focused more on doing the most two important laws of God consistently instead of having our slates clean and not committing ten any of the Ten Commandments, yet alone the most abdominal according to Christian belief?

I figured it to be this way, if I love God with my whole heart, the conviction of sin would weigh heavy on me in my distaste of hurting him. It would build a closer relationship with God focusing on just simply not hurting him. Some of us don't sin, but we don't love so we'll still go to hell. We don't steal or commit adultery but we can't stand our Pastor because He won't let us preach, so we wait for him to die not knowing that we have a seed of hate in our hearts. The most amazing thing about God is that our Lord commanded us to love. With God being our creator and sustainer, He knows our capabilities. So He commands us to do something that He is aware we have the capabilities to do. What type of creative creator would God be for him to create us inside out and command us to do something that He didn't give us the capability to do?

God gave us and our abilities to love, the power of control. Meaning you chose to hate them when your heart was capable of forgiveness. You decided to let hate rest and not deal with them. The saints have allowed themselves to believe that you can love someone and not like them. That is the most foolish cop-out one could preach. If I love you and dislike the things you do, then I am justified. God does not love us but dislike us. No, He loves us and dislikes the things that we do. Love has no escape doors or ways out if it's authentic. The Hebrew word for love known as "Chesed" or when Romanized "Khesed" would suggest that real love that remains steadfast is similar to serving to the point of abuse. It was like God's ticket for us to go higher and to the next level was love.

The qualification of your greatness was for you to go back with love and empower those that hurt you or destroyed you to this point of destiny. There is a remnant of leaders emerging in this generation who won't have the mic addiction similar to a man needing a blunt ad the pulpit won't be their crack house.

But God is restoring a group of people who have been through hell unmentionable but know the God called them, there is a generation of believers who have stared death in the face, but couldn't die because they were chosen. Everyone is sitting back wondering how and why you still even have breath in your body and your response is simple... "I love like God loves."

You can be ready for the ridicule and the shame of those who already didn't like you before this point but the key to your next level in God is to love those people until there is no end. God knew your story would be hurtful for you but helpful to the next individual. He favored you with individuality, not because you have a good personality but because your story is different. No one will talk about some of the same things you have gone through, but the fact would be that YOU ARE DIFFERENT! So not only did he give you the story but gave you're the courage to stand on the head of the devil and declare in the face of every mad preacher/pastor whose afraid, tormenting their empire, that the blood of Jesus will never go a lie and his blood reaches from to the highest mountain and it flows through the lowest valley.

It is the blood that gives us strength from day to day and it has never, is not, and will never lose its power! Learning to love like God gives us his charter. Loving in the emulation of God gives us his identity. Some of the church emulates God in appearance but we don't have his heart and love the way that he loves. The next generation of believers will exemplify God most through their ability to love like God more than look like him. In fact, those who love like him, look like him most. Your experiences cultivated you to not be a copycat but give you individual anointing to share universal love in order to compel people to a centralized God of love.

My life taught me that I had authority over my story! If the craziness that happens in real life is never confronted, then it can never be changed. It's like information without application gives you no complete transformation. My life happened for a reason and now it was time to be set up for a change. The old saints would say "I'm better because of the beating I didn't deserve." So we had to change our way of thinking so that our hearts could change. I couldn't let the pain of my past rob me of my desire to walk in destiny. The biggest and hardest lesson was to learn how to allow my pain to reposition me for purpose and allow pain to pay me.

Everything and everyone that I lost along the way, God was showing me that repossession was only for repositioning.

The issue was not with me, but with the people I went to. We need to be delivered from people who can't help folks who need to be delivered. You are gifted differently so you're tried differently, so now you can expect the devil to try you differently. You can expect the pain and pleasure out of every promise to push you into your greater potential. Your life was destined and God formulated an itinerary with you destiny as the destination. You won't get it because of everything you face today but as you progress into your season, there won't be any turning around.

It doesn't matter what you did, or how. The man at the pool of Bethesda, in Exodus 3:19, was stuck between a crisis and a promise but He was laced with the ferments of sin. But when his moment came, everything aligned to show that his day of grace had come. Imagine how he woke up that morning expecting to do business as usual. We had no clue he was a sinner until after his healing and deliverance. God strategically planned our failures and designed us to overcome even failure.

There is so much strength in every failure when you learn to get back up and keep going.

So the evening that I found myself experiencing God during bible study, years later, was only God showing me how He really did love me. How he kept me covered with Grace. He showed me how the prayers of the saints had covered me. Everything that looked like a problem was God only preparing me for greater. When we look at the life geological gospel of Christ, we see how he was from the hood, but called to change the hearts of all those important to come. He was talked about because of how different his ministry was. Jesus didn't preach hate but He lived love. The phrases or some modern day theologians call them church people, only disliked Jesus because his word was different from the practices they already had in place.

Learn to love even when it hurts and you'll began to notice how you look more and more like the Lord our God. Through absolutely everything, I learned prophetically that I am the reflection of God, created in his image and chosen to overcome all obstacles. I love each of you.....

God's letter to me (Poetic Expression)

I am the creator and the created. I am the

beginning and the end. I am the first and the last. I am the happy and the sad. I am life, yes the life that has good and bad. I am the Father and the Son. I am you and I am me. I am one with you and you can never be separate from me. I am always with you, I will never leave you, and in fact it's impossible for me too. So, lose the fear because I am always here and near to your heart. We are one, nothing can change that; not your past nor your present, not your sins nor your secrets. I am God. I am both the river and the ocean. I am both truth and love. I am also beyond both truth and love because words can't describe me. Truth and Love are just two of the best words to use when pointing to who I am. Who I am is unnamable, indescribable, and undeniable. Even in denying me you acknowledge me because it is impossible for I am to not be. But enough about me even though everything I said about me is true for you as well. Yes, Jesus is my child but you are as well. So denying him is denying me and when you deny yourself you are denying me as well, that's the same thing he told the "woman at the well." I love you so much how could I send you to hell? Let me say this again, did you see your brother Jesus and what he came to do? He showed you that you are me in physical form and the world is full of hate so please don't conform. See, when Jesus was born, King Herod tried to destroy all the newborns. So, I know all about child abuse but I am not making an excuse for their actions. During those moments you may have thought I was absent or distracted but you went through these things to become whole, this is only a fraction of the story. A story that brings me so much glory, glory that even Moses's story couldn't bring. After every fall and winter it's spring. So, even though you fell down you got back up. Now your cup runneth over and I want to repeat this over and over (life happens through seasons and everything that you experienced happened for a reason.) Your life is a testimony, this is the Book of Ephesians. But it's a shame that the same people who deny you accepts King James; who was allegedly homosexual, liar, murderer, thief, and one of the biggest slaves masters in the southeast. So, please be at peace, your past doesn't negate the fact that I have called you to preach. This isn't a campaign and you can't get impeached. My anointing is upon you; you can't imagine the heights you will reach, the places you will teach, the souls you will make meek. Your story alone will inspire nations and be the inspiration to everyone who is in your situation. You have been through periods of confusion and insulation but today is your graduation. This is the confirmation of your liberation. I am pleased with your transformation.

Therefore, your life will be the illustration.

Congratulations my son, you found yourself. When

you found you, you found me. I am God, I am

greater than HIV. I have revealed my power to you

when I healed you. I healed you from HIV. My son,

let me say that again, I healed you from HIV. To

human it's major but it wasn't a big deal to me.

Because, you yielded to me and kneeled to me. Your

faith has restored you. Therefore, everything you

touch will be healed by your faith. My son, you have

my grace, you have endured the race, you have

sought my face, and now you must take your place.

You are healing, healing is your identity. Now your

life is an entity and ministry that will impact this

world tremendously. Healing and Love is who you

are. Healing and Love is who you are. Healing and

Love is who you are. You are Mozart because your

presence will be as peaceful as a violin. Suicide was knocking at your door but you didn't let it in. No my son you didn't give in, you kept the faith and you went within, and repented of your sins. And the healing of HIV did indeed begin. Although, some people may not believe, they are just like the Pharisees, they didn't believe Jesus when he healed leprosy. That's hypocrisy religion has become a terrible democracy. But this is more than an autobiography this is modern-day theology. You are me and that's not reverse psychology nor is it an apology. YOU ARE LOVE. Don't you know it's all about you to me? Because, you give it up for me and I give it up for you, when you look in the mirror what do you see? You see a reflection an image of what you call me and that's the same thing I see when I look at your heart. You are just like me and you were from the start. So don't deny your greatness, you are a reflection of me and in me

there is no fake-ness. Awaken please to your song,

you are my young king and your heart is my home.

You are spirit in a body, love in the flesh. I am God

in you, God in the flesh. So don't focus on mess and

get stuck in earthly stress, you are amazing don't

you ever forget that. Although, religious people may

call you lost, in order for something to be found it

first has to be lost. All the pain you been through

your mentally died on the cross. But I resurrected

your identity, now you are changed for infinity. You

are one, complete, and whole like the Holy Trinity.

You will reach more people than John F. Kennedy.

You have tapped into your Divinity and calmed your

hostility with the flesh. But even when you were in

sin you were never less than what I called you to be.

I elected you, selected you, and perfected you. Now

go be what I have called you to be!!!!! (P.S. Never

forget YOU ARE LOVE. When I look at you, I am all I see. Therefore, you are one of a kind and if you wasn't I wouldn't call you mine. Because everything I created is perfectly designed. I created you to make mistakes that's what it takes to grow and evolve. I made you and you are here on earth to make my love, my healing, and my greatness known and please don't ever forget YOUR HEART IS MY HOME!) -From God

By- Truth iTellit (Raymond Jr.)